YOU ARE

A BADASS

EVERYDAY

A LOT OF MOTIVATION

IN A LITTLE BOOK

D1563911

By

JONNY KATZ

TABLE OF CONTENTS

CONQUER FEAR AND NEVER GIVE UP

Never let the fear of striking out keep you from playing the game.

— Babe Ruth

Everything you've ever wanted is on the other side of fear.

— George Addair

Don't be pushed around by the fears in your mind. Be led by the dreams in your heart.

Roy T. Bennett

Instead of worrying about what you cannot control, shift your energy to what you can create.

— Roy T. Bennett

Courage

Whatever you do, you need courage.

Whatever course you decide upon, there is always someone to tell you that you are wrong.

There are always difficulties arising that tempt you to believe your critics are right.

To map out a course of action and follow it to an end requires some of the same courage that a soldier needs.

Peace has its victories,

but it takes brave men and women to win them.

— Ralph Waldo Emerson

· • — — · ❖ · — — • ·

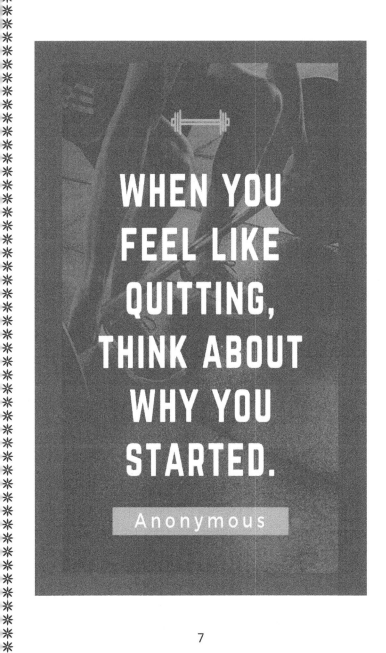

WHEN YOU FEEL LIKE QUITTING, THINK ABOUT WHY YOU STARTED.

Anonymous

He who has conquered doubt and fear has conquered failure.

— James Lane Allen

He who fears being conquered is sure of defeat.

— Napoleon Bonaparte

I am not afraid; I was born to do this.

— Joan of Arc

Cowards die many times before their deaths; the valiant never taste of death but once.

— William Shakespeare

Live! Live the wonderful life that is in you! Let nothing be lost upon you. Be always searching for new sensations. Be afraid of nothing.

— Oscar Wilde

It is stupidity rather than courage to refuse to recognize danger when it is close upon you.

— Arthur Conan Doyle

A man with outward courage dares to die; a man with inner courage dares to live.

— Lao Tzu

The true courage is in facing danger when you are afraid, and that kind of courage you have in plenty.

— L. Frank Baum

We gain strength, and courage, and confidence by each experience in which we really stop to look fear in the face... we must do that which we think we cannot.

— Eleanor Roosevelt

Do one thing every day that scares you.

— Eleanor Roosevelt

· • — — · ✚ · — — • .***

Always do what you are afraid to do.

— Ralph Waldo Emerson

· • — — · ✚ · — — • ·

It's not enough to be nice in life. You've got to have nerve.

— Georgia O'Keeffe

· • — — · ✚ · — — • ·

It's not enough to be nice in life. You've got to have nerve.

— Georgia O'Keeffe

· • — — · ✚ · — — • ·

"When tempted to fight fire with fire, remember that the Fire Department usually uses water." - Unknown

· • — — · ❖ · — — • ·

If you want to count for something more than the average. Let every obstacle be a fresh incentive to action.

— Anonymous

· • — — · ❖ · — — • ·

Do what you feel in your heart to be right — for you'll be criticized anyway.

— Eleanor Roosevelt

· • — — · ❖ · — — • ·

Nothing in life is to be feared. It is only to be understood.

— Marie Curie

· • — — · ❖ · — — •

The purpose of life is to live it, to taste experience to the utmost, to reach out eagerly and without fear for newer and richer experience.

— Eleanor Roosevelt

It is not death that a man should fear, but he should fear never beginning to live.

— Marcus Aurelius

A person who never made a mistake never tried anything new.

— Albert Einstein

Life can be wonderful if you're not afraid of it. All it takes is courage, imagination ... and a little dough.

— Charlie Chaplin

EMBRACE CHANGE

It's only after you've stepped outside your comfort zone that you begin to change, grow, and transform.

— Roy T. Bennett

The secret of change is to focus all of your energy, not on fighting the old, but on building the new

— Socrates

Your mind is a powerful thing. When you fill it with positive thoughts, your life will start to change

— Gautama Buddha

The most useless are those who never change through the years...

— James M. Barrie

The most useless are those who never change through the years…

— James M. Barrie

There are only two ways to live your life. One is as though nothing is a miracle. The other is as though everything is a miracle.

— Albert Einstein

Cautious, careful people, always casting about to preserve their reputations... can never effect a reform.

— Susan B. Anthony

Be the change that you wish to see in the world.

— Mahatma Gandhi

See it Through

When you're up against a trouble,
*   Meet it squarely, face to face;*
Lift your chin and set your shoulders,
*   Plant your feet and take a brace.*
When it's vain to try to dodge it,
*   Do the best that you can do;*
You may fail, but you may conquer,
*   See it through!*

Black may be the clouds about you
*   And your future may seem grim,*
But don't let your nerve desert you;
*   Keep yourself in fighting trim.*
If the worst is bound to happen,
*   Spite of all that you can do,*
Running from it will not save you,
*   See it through!*

Even hope may seem but futile,
*   When with troubles you're beset,*
But remember you are facing
*   Just what other men have met.*
You may fail, but fall still fighting;

15

Don't give up, whate'er you do;
Eyes front, head high to the finish.
See it through!

by Edgar Albert Guest

· • — — · ✤ · — — • ·

Never doubt that a small group of thoughtful, committed, citizens can change the world. Indeed, it is the only thing that ever has.

— Margaret Mead

· • — — · ✤ · — — • ·

Change is the law of life. And those who look only to the past or present are certain to miss the future.

—John F. Kennedy

· • — — · ✤ · — — • ·

Not Lie at Anchor

I find the great thing in this world is
Not so much where we stand,
As in what direction we are moving.
To reach the port of Heaven,
We must sail sometimes with the wind
And sometimes against it, —
But we must sail, and not drift,
Nor lie at anchor.

by Oliver Wendell Holmes

· • — — · ♣ · — — • ·

You never change things by fighting the existing reality. To change something, build a new model that makes the existing model obsolete.

—Buckminster Fuller

If you always do what you've always done, you'll always get what you've always got."

—Henry Ford

· • — — · ✤ · — — • ·

Be Done with It

Finish every day and be done with it.
You have done what you could;
Some blunders and absurdities no doubt crept in;
Forget them as soon as you can.

Tomorrow is a new day;
You shall begin it well and serenely
And with too high a spirit
To be cumbered with your old nonsense.

by Ralph Waldo Emerson

· • — — · ✤ · — — • ·

To exist is to change, to change is to mature, to mature is to go on creating oneself endlessly."

—Henri Bergson

· • — — · ✤ · — — • ·

FIND YOUR PURPOSE AND ACHIEVE
YOUR DREAMS

The secret of getting ahead is getting started

— Mark Twain

Go confidently in the direction of your dreams.
Live the life you have imagined

— Henry David Thoreau

Knowing is not enough; we must apply.
Wishing is not enough; we must do.

— Johann Wolfgang von Goethe

The only limit to our realization of tomorrow
will be our doubts of today.

— Franklin D. Roosevelt

Self Control

On my finger I tied a string
To help me remember things
Every day I set a goal
Today my goal is self—control

We're faced with choices, says my dad
Choices to do good or bad
In the end what will you choose?
To win with good or will you lose?

There are some things that seem like fun
That end up wrong when all is done.
Like sometimes
I want to touch wet paint
Or stick my fingers in the cake

But then I look down at my string
And I choose not to do these things
My string helped me achieve my goal
I'm glad that I learned self—control

by Anonymous

· • — — · ❖ · — — • ·

Twenty years from now, you will be more disappointed by the things that you didn't do than by the ones you did do. So, throw off the bowlines, sail away from the safe harbor, catch the trade winds in your sails. Explore, Dream, Discover.

— Mark Twain

· • —— · ♣ · —— • ·

First, have a definite, clear, practical ideal; a goal, an objective. Second, have the necessary means to achieve your ends; wisdom, money, materials, and methods. Third, adjust all your means to that end.

— Aristotle

· • —— · ♣ · —— • ·

You are never too old to set another goal or to dream a new dream.

— C.S. Lewis

Try Again

It's a lesson you should heed,
Try, try again.

If at first you don't succeed,
Try, try again.
Then your courage should appear,
For if you will persevere,
You will conquer, never fear,
Try, try again.

Once or twice, though you should fail,
Try, try again.

If you would at last prevail,
Try, try again

If we strive, 'tis no disgrace,
Though we do not win the race;
What should you do in that case?
Try, try again.

If you find your task is hard,
Try, try again.

Time will bring you your reward,
Try, try again

All that other folk can do,
Why, with patience, should not you?
Only keep this rule in view, Try, try again.

by William Edward Hickson

· ● — — · ❖ · — — ● ·

Our greatest glory is not in never falling, but in rising every time we fall

— Confucius

· ● — — · ❖ · — — ● ·

When everything seems to be going against you, remember that the airplane takes off against the wind, not with it

— Henry Ford

· ● — — · ❖ · — — ● ·

The two most important days in your life are the day you are born and the day you find out why.

— Mark Twain

Don't let yesterday take up too much of today

— Will Rogers

Go confidently in the direction of your dreams! Live the life you've imagined

— Henry David Thoreau

Whatever you can do, or dream you can, begin it. Boldness has genius, power and magic in it.

—Johann Wolfgang von Goethe

Carpe diem! Rejoice while you are alive; enjoy the day; live life to the fullest; make the most of what you have. It is later than you think.

— Horace

DREAMS

Hold fast to dreams
For if dreams die
Life is a broken-winged bird
That cannot fly.
Hold fast to dreams
For when dreams go
Life is a barren field
Frozen with snow.

Langston Hughes

Every strike brings me closer to the next home run.

— Babe Ruth

If the wind will not serve, take to the oars.

—Latin Proverb

The best way to predict your future is to create it…

— Abraham Lincoln

The beginning is the most important part of the work…

— Plato

The achievement of one goal should be the starting point of another.

— Alexander Graham Bell

It Couldn't Be Done

Somebody said that it couldn't be done
*   But he with a chuckle replied*
That maybe it couldn't, but he would be one
*   Who wouldn't say so till he'd tried.*
So he buckled right in with the trace of a grin
*   On his face. If he worried he hid it.*
He started to sing as he tackled the thing
*   That couldn't be done, and he did it!*

Somebody scoffed: Oh, you'll never do that;
*   At least no one ever has done it;*
But he took off his coat and he took off his hat
*   And the first thing we knew he'd begun it.*
With a lift of his chin and a bit of a grin,
*   Without any doubting or quiddit,*
He started to sing as he tackled the thing
*   That couldn't be done, and he did it.*

There are thousands to tell you it cannot be done,
*   There are thousands to prophesy failure,*
There are thousands to point out to you one by one,
*   The dangers that wait to assail you.*
But just buckle in with a bit of a grin,
*   Just take off your coat and go to it;*
Just start in to sing as you tackle the thing
*   That cannot be done, and you'll do it.*

by Edgar Albert Guest

You have to run as fast as you can just to stay where you are. If you want to get anywhere, you'll have to run much faster.

— Lewis Carroll

You gain strength, courage, and confidence by doing the thing which you think you cannot do.

— Eleanor Roosevelt

The future belongs to those who believe in the beauty of their dreams.

— Eleanor Roosevelt

Start by doing what's necessary; then do what's possible; and suddenly you are doing the impossible.

— Francis of Assisi

Only those who attempt the absurd can achieve the impossible.

— Albert Einstein

Great minds have purposes, others have wishes.

– Washington Irving

The best way to lengthen out our days is to walk steadily and with a purpose.

– Charles Dickens

The mystery of human existence lies not in just staying alive, but in finding something to live for."

– Fyodor Dostoyevsky

It is not enough to be industrious; so are the ants. What are you industrious about?

— Henry David Thoreau

HAPPINESS, FRIENDSHIP, AND LOVE

Don't walk behind me; I may not lead. Don't walk in front of me; I may not follow. Just walk beside me and be my friend.

— Albert Camus

Good friends, good books and a sleepy conscience: this is the ideal life.

Mark Twain

What do we live for, if it is not to make life less difficult for each other?

— George Eliot

When you're alone you don't do much laughing.

— **P.G. Wodehouse**

Sometimes our light goes out, but is blown again into instant flame by an encounter with another human being.

— Albert Schweitzer

Love is that condition in which the happiness of another person is essential to your own.

— Robert A. Heinlein

"As we grow older and realize more clearly the limitations of human happiness, we come to see that the only real and abiding pleasure in life is to give pleasure to other people."
— P.G. Wodehouse,

Happiness resides not in possessions, and not in gold, happiness dwells in the soul.

— Democritus

There is only one way to happiness and that is to cease worrying about things which are beyond the power of our will.

— Epictetus

Derive happiness in oneself from a good day's work, from illuminating the fog that surrounds us.

— Henri Matisse

Take responsibility of your own happiness, never put it in other people's hands.

— Roy T. Bennett

Be the reason someone smiles. Be the reason someone feels loved and believes in the goodness in people.

— Roy T. Bennett

More smiling, less worrying. More compassion, less judgment. More blessed, less stressed. More love, less hate.

— Roy T. Bennett

Creativity is intelligence having fun

— Albert Einstein

Rules for Happiness: something to do, someone to love, something to hope for.

— Immanuel Kant

Let us be grateful to people who make us happy, they are the charming gardeners who make our souls blossom.

— Marcel Proust

Happiness depends more on the inward disposition of mind than on outward circumstances.

— Benjamin Franklin

The human race has one really effective weapon, and that is laughter.

— Mark Twain

Do not take life too seriously. You will never get out of it alive…

— Elbert Hubbard

Happiness doesn't depend on what we have, but it does depend on how we feel toward what we have. We can be happy with little and miserable with much. — William D. Hoard

The best and most beautiful things in the world cannot be seen or even touched — they must be felt with the heart — Helen Keller

Whoever is happy will make others happy too — Anne Frank

· • — — · ✣ · — — • ·

Do not spoil what you have by desiring what you have not; remember that what you now have was once among the things you only hoped for. — Epicurus

· • — — · ✣ · — — • ·

The purpose of our lives is to be happy

— Dalai Lama

· • — — · ✣ · — — • ·

Spread love everywhere you go. Let no one ever come to you without leaving happier

— Mother Teresa

I would rather die of passion than of boredom

— Vincent van Gogh

Love the life you live. Live the life you love

Bob Marley

There is nothing on this earth more to be prized than true friendship.

—St. Thomas Aquinas

When one door of happiness closes, another opens, but often we look so long at the closed door that we do not see the one that has been opened for us.

—Helen Keller

Happiness is not something ready—made. It comes from your own actions.

—Dalai Lama

Trust yourself. Create the kind of self that you will be happy to live with all your life. Make the most of yourself by fanning the tiny, inner sparks of possibility into flames of achievement.

— Golda Meir

Sometimes your joy is the source of your smile, but sometimes your smile can be the source of your joy.

— Nhat Hanh

True happiness is to enjoy the present, without anxious dependence on the future.

— Seneca

For every minute you are angry you lose sixty seconds of happiness…

— Ralph Waldo Emerson

The secret of happiness is to admire without desiring.

— Carl Sandburg

The best way to cheer yourself up is to try to cheer somebody else up.

— Mark Twain

The fact is always obvious much too late, but the most singular difference between happiness and joy is that happiness is a solid and joy a liquid.

— J.D. Salinger

Always laugh when you can. It is cheap medicine.

— Lord Byron

I am a happy camper so I guess I'm doing something right. Happiness is like a butterfly; the more you chase it, the more it will elude you, but if you turn your attention to other things, it will come and sit softly on your shoulder.

— Henry David Thoreau

Happiness is a gift and the trick is not to expect it, but to delight in it when it comes.

— Charles Dickens

Happiness belongs to the self—sufficient.

— Aristotle

If you want others to be happy, practice compassion. If you want to be happy, practice compassion.

— Dalai Lama

The things that we love tell us what we are.

— St. Thomas Aquinas

The noblest pleasure is the joy of understanding…

— Leonardo da Vinci

Happiness is when what you think, what you say, and what you do are in harmony.

— Mahatma Gandhi

Be happy. It's one way of being wise.

— Sidonie Colette

Love inspires, illuminates, designates and leads the way.

— Mary Baker Eddy

Do not speak of your happiness to one less fortunate than yourself.

— Plutarch

Happiness is not a goal; it is a by—product.

— Eleanor Roosevelt

Happiness is not a possession to be prized, it is a quality of thought, a state of mind.

— Daphne du Maurier

Some cause happiness wherever they go; others, whenever they go.

— Oscar Wilde

The U.S. Constitution doesn't guarantee happiness, only the pursuit of it. You have to catch up with it yourself.

— Benjamin Franklin

Happiness lies not in the mere possession of money; it lies in the joy of achievement, in the thrill of creative effort.

— Franklin D. Roosevelt

I, not events, have the power to make me happy or unhappy today. I can choose which it shall be. Yesterday is dead, tomorrow hasn't arrived yet. I have just one day, today, and I'm going to be happy in it.

— Groucho Marx

Love all, trust a few, do wrong to none.

— William Shakespeare

Most folks are as happy as they make up their minds to be.

— Abraham Lincoln

Thousands of candles can be lighted from a single candle. Happiness never decreases by being shared.

— Gautama Buddha

In friendship, as in love, we are often happier through our ignorance than our knowledge.

— William Shakespeare

Happiness is not to be found in knowledge, but in the acquisition of knowledge.

— Edgar Allan Poe

Love does not see with the eyes, but with the soul.

— William Shakespeare

Kindness in women, not their beauteous looks, shall win my love.

— William Shakespeare

Piglet: How do you spell 'love'?
Winnie the Pooh: You don't spell it...you feel it.

— A.A. Milne

A light heart lives long.

— William Shakespeare

It is a happiness to wonder; it is a happiness to dream.

— Edgar Allan Poe

A little misery, at times, makes one appreciate happiness more.

— L. Frank Baum

That pleasure which is at once the most pure, the most elevating, and the most intense, is derived, I maintain, from the contemplation of the beautiful.

— Edgar Allan Poe

Work is the best antidote to sorrow, my dear Watson.

— Arthur Conan Doyle

When you are good to others, you are best to yourself.

— Benjamin Franklin

· • — — · ❖ · — — • ·

Laughing Song

When the green woods laugh with the voice of joy,
And the dimpling stream runs laughing by;
When the air does laugh with our merry wit,
And the green hill laughs with the noise of it;

when the meadows laugh with lively green,
And the grasshopper laughs in the merry scene,
When Mary and Susan and Emily
With their sweet round mouths sing Ha, ha he!

When the painted birds laugh in the shade,
Where our table with cherries and nuts is spread:
Come live, and be merry, and join with me,
To sing the sweet chorus of Ha, ha, he!

by William Blake

· • — — · ❖ · — — • ·

Independence is happiness.

— Susan B. Anthony

· • — — · ✜ · — — • ·

Action may not always bring happiness, but there is no happiness without action.

— William James

· • — — · ✜ · — — • ·

Peace begins with a smile.

— Mother Teresa

· • — — · ✜ · — — • ·

The power of finding beauty in the humblest things makes home happy and life lovely.

— Louisa May Alcott

· • — — · ✜ · — — • ·

I've had a lot of worries in my life, most of which never happened.

— Mark Twain

· • — — · ✜ · — — • ·

There is no happiness like that of being loved by your fellow creatures, and feeling that your presence is an addition to their comfort.

— Charlotte Brontë,

· • — — · ✤ · — — • ·

The habit of being happy enables one to be freed, or largely freed, from the domination of outward conditions.

Robert Louis Stevenson

A Smile

Smiling is infectious.
You catch it like the flu,
When someone smiled at me today,
I started smiling too.

I passed around the corner,
And someone saw my grin,
When he smiled, I realized,
I'd passed it on to him.

I thought about that smile,
Then realized its worth,
A single smile, just like mine,
Could travel round the earth.

So, if you feel a smile begin,
Don't leave it undetected.
Let's start an epidemic quick,
And get the world infected.

Author Unknown

· • — — · ✢ · — — • ·

ABOUT LIFE AND THE FUTURE

Attitude is a choice. Happiness is a choice. Optimism is a choice. Kindness is a choice. Giving is a choice. Respect is a choice. Whatever choice you make makes you. Choose wisely.

— Roy T. Bennett

It is a good rule in life never to apologize. The right sort of people do not want apologies, and the wrong sort take a mean advantage of them.

— P.G. Wodehouse

Life is too short to waste your time on people who don't respect, appreciate, and value you.

— Roy T. Bennett

It's during our darkest moments that we must focus to see the light

— Aristotle

I Know

One time I thought I knew it all
But now I must confess
The more I know I know I know
I know I know the less.

by Anonymous

If you want to be happy, do not dwell in the past, do not worry about the future, focus on living fully in the present.

— Roy T. Bennett

I alone cannot change the world, but I can cast a stone across the water to create many ripples

— Mother Teresa

Stopping by the Woods

Whose woods these are I think I know.
His house is in the village though;
He will not see me stopping here
To watch his woods fill up with snow.
My little horse must think it queer
To stop without a farmhouse near
Between the woods and frozen lake
The darkest evening of the year.
He gives his harness bells a shake
To ask if there is some mistake.
The only other sound's the sweep
Of easy wind and downy flake.
The woods are lovely, dark and deep.
But I have promises to keep,
And miles to go before I sleep,
And miles to go before I sleep.

— by Robert Frost

· ● — — · ✤ · — — ● ·

Don't judge each day by the harvest you reap
but by the seeds that you plant

— Robert Louis Stevenson

Hope – Winston Churchill

Smiles from the threshold of the year to come,
Whispering 'it will be happier'.

— Alfred Lord Tennyson

Keep your face always toward the sunshine and
shadows will fall behind you

— Walt Whitman

· • — — · ❖ · — — • ·

The pessimist sees difficulty in every
opportunity. The optimist sees opportunity in
every difficulty

— Winston Churchill

· • — — · ❖ · — — • ·

"Never put off until tomorrow
what you can do the day
after tomorrow."
- Mark Twain

Don't waste your time in anger, regrets, worries, and grudges. Life is too short to be unhappy.

— Roy T. Bennett

· • — — · ✣ · — — • ·

Life is never fair. And perhaps it is a good thing for most of us that it is not

— Oscar Wilde

· • — — · ✣ · — — • ·

In the end, it's not the years in your life that count. It's the life in your years

— Abraham Lincoln

· • -- · ✣ · -- • ·

Hope – by Emily Dickinson

Hope is the thing with feathers
That perches in the soul,
And sings the tune without the words,
And never stops at all,

And sweetest in the gale is heard;
And sore must be the storm
That could abash the little bird
That kept so many warm.

I've heard it in the chillest land,
And on the strangest sea;
Yet, never, in extremity,
It asked a crumb of me.

by Emily Dickinson

"Unseen in the background,
Fate was quietly
slipping lead
into the boxing-glove."

P.G. Wodehouse

· • — — · ✤ · — — • ·

Auguries of Innocence

To see a World in a Grain of Sand
And a Heaven in a Wild Flower,
Hold Infinity in the palm of your hand
And Eternity in an hour.

By William Blake

· • — — · ✤ · — — • ·

Life is either a daring adventure or nothing at all.

— Helen Keller

Live in the sunshine, swim the sea, drink the wild air

— Ralph Waldo Emerson

Life is ours to be spent, not to be saved

— D. H. Lawrence

The Inner Side

The inner side of every cloud
Is bright and shining;
I therefore turn my clouds about,
And always wear them inside out,
To show the lining.

by Ellen Thorneycroft Fowler

In three words, I can sum up everything I've learned about life: it goes on

— Robert Frost

Life itself is the most wonderful fairy tale

— Hans Christian Anderson

The best time to plant a tree was 20 years ago. The second—best time is now.

—Chinese Proverb

An unexamined life is not worth living.

—Socrates

Life is a balance of holding on and letting go…
— Rumi

Life shrinks or expands in proportion to one's courage.

—Anais Nin

How wonderful it is that nobody need wait a single moment before starting to improve the world.

—Anne Frank

Life is short, Break the Rules. Forgive quickly, Kiss slowly. Love truly. Laugh uncontrollably. And never regret ANYTHING That makes you smile.

— Mark Twain

Life. is a festival only to the wise.

— Ralph Waldo Emerson

Life is a tale told by an idiot — full of sound and fury, signifying nothing…

— William Shakespeare

Life is about accepting the challenges along the way, choosing to keep moving forward, and savoring the journey.

— Roy T. Bennett

You can't build a reputation on what you are going to do.

— Henry Ford

Life is not meant to be easy, my child; but take courage: it can be delightful.

— George Bernard Shaw

Be comforted, dear soul! There is always light behind the clouds.

— Louisa May Alcott

· • — — · ♣ · — — • ·

I look to the future because that's where I'm going to spend the rest of my life.

— George Burns

· • — — · ♣ · — — • ·

The
FUTURE
depends on
what we do
in the
PRESENT.
Mahatma Gandhi

STILL HERE

I been scarred and battered.
My hopes the wind done scattered.
Snow has friz me,
Sun has baked me,
Looks like between 'em they done
Tried to make me
Stop laughin', stop lovin', stop
livin'–
But I don't care!
I'm still here!

Langston Hughes

· • — · ✤ · — • ·

Well, everyone can master a grief but he that has it.

— William Shakespeare

Life is infinitely stranger than anything which the mind of man could invent.

— Arthur Conan Doyle

There are times, young fellah, when every one of us must make a stand for human right and justice, or you never feel clean again.

— Arthur Conan Doyle

· • — — · ✤ · — — • ·

If you limit your actions in life to things that nobody can possibly find fault with, you will not do much!

— Lewis Carroll

· • — — · ✤ · — — • ·

The purpose of life is to live it, to taste experience to the utmost, to reach out eagerly and without fear for newer and richer experience.

— Eleanor Roosevelt

But you will admit that it's a good thing to be alive.

— L. Frank Baum

The future is literally in our hands to mold as we like. But we cannot wait until tomorrow. Tomorrow is now.

— Eleanor Roosevelt

Most of us tiptoe through life in order to make it safely to death.

— Theodore Roosevelt

Live as if you were to die tomorrow. Learn as if you were to live forever.

— Mahatma Gandhi

May you live every day of your life.

— Jonathan Swift

The meaning of life is to find your gift. The purpose of life is to give it away.

— Pablo Picasso

Life is not easy for any of us. But what of that? We must have perseverance and above all confidence in ourselves. We must believe that we are gifted for something, and that this thing, at whatever cost, must be attained.

— Marie Curie

You can't stay in your corner of the Forest waiting for others to come to you. You have to go to them sometimes.

— A.A. Milne

To live is the rarest thing in the world. Most people exist, that is all.

— Oscar Wilde

Life was meant to be lived, and curiosity must be kept alive. One must never, for whatever reason, turn his back on life.

— Eleanor Roosevelt

Life is like riding a bicycle. To keep your balance, you must keep moving.

— Albert Einstein

The greatest danger for most of us is not that our aim is too high and we miss it, but that it is too low and we reach it.

— Michelangelo

Any idiot can face a crisis — it's day to day living that wears you out.

— Anton Chekhov

The person who has lived the most is not the one with the most years but the one with the richest experiences.

— Jean-Jacques Rousseau

Anyone who stops learning is old, whether at twenty or eighty. Anyone who keeps learning stays young. The greatest thing in life is to keep your mind young.

— Henry Ford

How far you go in life depends on your being tender with the young, compassionate with the aged, sympathetic with the striving and tolerant of the weak and strong. Because someday in your life you will have been all of these.

— George Washington Carver

Only you can control your future.

— Dr. Seuss

We are called to be architects of the future, not its victims.

— R. Buckminster Fuller

I don't believe in regrets; I believe your future is in your tomorrows.

— John Travolta

SUCCESS AND FAILURE

The best thing about the future is that it comes one day at a time.

—Abraham Lincoln

The most difficult thing is the decision to act; the rest is merely tenacity

— Amelia Earhart

Whether you think you can or think you can't, you're right

— Henry Ford

Success is not how high you have climbed, but how you make a positive difference to the world.

— Roy T. Bennett

Thinking

If you think you are beaten, you are
If you think you dare not, you don't,
If you like to win, but you think you can'
It is almost certain you won't.

If you think you'll lose, you're lost
For out of the world we find,
Success begins with a fellow's will
It's all in the state of mind.

If you think you are outclassed, you are
You've got to think high to rise,
You've got to be sure of yourself before
You can ever win a prize.

Life's battles don't always go
To the stronger or faster man,
But soon or late the man who wins
Is the man WHO THINKS HE CAN!

Walter D. Wintle

· • — — · ✣ · — — • ·

Believe you can, and you're halfway there.

— Theodore Roosevelt

· • — — · ✣ · — — • ·

Always bear in mind that your own resolution to success is more important than any other one thing.

— Abraham Lincoln

· • — — · ✣ · — — • ·

"The road to success is dotted with many tempting parking spaces."
- Will Rogers

· • — — · ✣ · — — • ·

I find that the harder I work, the more luck I seem to have.

— Thomas Jefferson

· • — — · ✣ · — — • ·

Success is walking from failure to failure with no loss of enthusiasm

— Winston Churchill

I attribute my success to this: I never gave or took any excuse

— Florence Nightingale

A Noble Life

Wouldst shape a noble life?
Then cast No backward glance toward the past,
And though somewhat be lost and gone,
Yet do thou act as one new born;
What each day needs, that shalt thou ask.
Each day will set its proper task.

by Johann Wolfgang von Goethe

Success usually comes to those who are too busy to be looking for it

— Henry David Thoreau

Success is not final; failure is not fatal: it is the courage to continue that counts

— Winston S. Churchill

Failure will never overtake me if my determination to succeed is strong enough

— Og Mandino

Many of life's failures are people who did not realize how close they were to success when they gave up

— Thomas A. Edison

When you reach the end of your rope, tie a knot in it and hang on

— Franklin D. Roosevelt

It is better to fail in originality than to succeed in imitation — Herman Melville

There is only one way to avoid criticism: do nothing, say nothing, and be nothing.

—Aristotle

Fall seven times and stand up eight.

—Japanese Proverb

You can't fall if you don't climb. But there's no joy in living your whole life on the ground.

—Unknown

I didn't fail the test. I just found 100 ways to do it wrong.

—Benjamin Franklin

The person who says it cannot be done should not interrupt the person who is doing it.

—Chinese Proverb

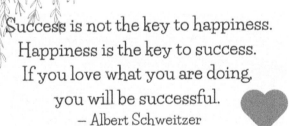

Success is not the key to happiness.
Happiness is the key to success.
If you love what you are doing,
you will be successful.
– Albert Schweitzer

The only difference between success and failure is the ability to take action.

— Alexander Graham Bell

There are many roads to success, but only one sure road to failure; and that is to try to please everyone else.

— Benjamin Franklin

I attribute my whole success in life to a rigid observance of the fundamental rule — Never have yourself tattooed with any woman's name, not even her initials.

— P.G. Wodehouse

Excellence is never an accident. It is always the result of high intention, sincere effort, and intelligent execution; it represents the wise choice of many alternatives — choice, not chance, determines your destiny.

— Aristotle

I attribute my success to this — I never gave or took any excuse.

— Florence Nightingale

· • —— · ✤ · —— • ·

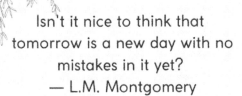

Isn't it nice to think that tomorrow is a new day with no mistakes in it yet?
— L.M. Montgomery

· • —— · ✤ · —— • ·

Always bear in mind that your own resolution to succeed is more important than any one thing.

— Abraham Lincoln

· • —— · ✤ · —— • ·

Dripping water hollows out stone, not through force but through persistence.

— Ovid

· • —— · ✤ · —— • ·

Great things are not done by impulse, but by a series of small things brought together.

— Vincent Van Gogh

You can't turn back the clock. But you can wind it up again.

— Bonnie Prudden

Finish each day and be done with it. You have done what you could. Some blunders and absurdities no doubt crept in; forget them as soon as you can. Tomorrow is a new day; begin it well and serenely and with too high a spirit to be encumbered with your old nonsense.

— Ralph Waldo Emerson

· • — — · ❖ · — — • ·

Be yourself, everyone else is already taken

— Oscar Wilde

· • — — · ❖ · — — • ·

There are far, far better things ahead than any we leave behind.

— C. S. Lewis

The more you believed in yourself, the more you could trust yourself. The more you trust yourself, the less you compare yourself to others.

— Roy T. Bennett

Think like a proton. Always positive.

– Unknown

You can't wait for inspiration. You have to go after it with a club.

– Jack London

BELIEVE IN YOURSELF

Accept yourself, love yourself, and keep moving forward. If you want to fly, you have to give up what weighs you down.

— Roy T. Bennett

It is never too late to be what you might have been

— George Eliot

I am not always good and noble. I am the hero of this story, but I have my off moments.

— P.G. Wodehouse

Always remember that you are absolutely unique. Just like everyone else

— Margaret Mead

The only person you are destined to become is the person you decide to be

— Ralph Waldo Emerson

The man who has confidence in himself gains the confidence of others

— Hasidic Proverb

Try not to become a person of success, but rather, try to become a person of value

— Albert Einstein

We are what we repeatedly do. Excellence, then, is not an act, but a habit

— Aristotle

Invictus

Out of the night that covers me,
Black as the Pit from pole to pole,
I thank whatever gods may be
For my unconquerable soul.

In the fell clutch of circumstance
I have not winced nor cried aloud,
Under the bludgeonings of chance
My head is bloody, but unbowed.

Beyond this place of wrath and tears
Looms but the horror of the shade,
And yet the menace of the years
Finds, and shall find me, unafraid.

It matters not how strait the gate,
How charged with punishments the scroll,
I am the master of my fate:
I am the captain of my soul.

By W.E. Henley

· • — — · ❖ · — — • ·

No one can make you feel inferior without your consent

— Eleanor Roosevelt

If life were predictable, it would cease to be life, and be without flavor

— Eleanor Roosevelt

I always advise people never to give advice.

— P.G. Wodehouse

The mind is everything. What you think you become.

—Buddha

Every child is an artist. The problem is how to remain an artist once he grows up.

—Pablo Picasso

If you hear a voice within you say you cannot paint, then by all means paint and that voice will be silenced.

—Vincent Van Gogh

We must believe that we are gifted for something, and that this thing, at whatever cost, must be attained.

—Marie Curie

Believe in yourself. You are braver than you think, more talented than you know, and capable of more than you imagine.

— Roy T. Bennett

Do you want to know who you are? Don't ask. Act! Action will delineate and define you.

— Thomas Jefferson

Tis in ourselves that we are thus or thus. Our bodies are our gardens to the which our wills are gardeners.

— William Shakespeare

You yourself as much as anybody in the entire universe deserve your love and affection.

— Gautama Buddha

He is able who think he is able.

— Gautama Buddha

Whatever you are, be a good one.

— Abraham Lincoln

If we are true to ourselves, we cannot be false to anyone.

— William Shakespeare

· • — — · ❖ · — — • ·

It is not in the stars to hold our destiny but in ourselves.

— William Shakespeare

· • — — · ❖ · — — • ·

To 'know Thyself' is considered quite an accomplishment.

— L. Frank Baum

· • — — · ❖ · — — • ·

A man, as a general rule, owes very little to what he is born with — a man is what he makes of himself.

— Alexander Graham Bell

· • — — · ❖ · — — • ·

Promise me you'll always remember: You're braver than you believe, and stronger than you seem, and smarter than you think.

— A.A. Milne

· • — — · ❖ · — — • ·

Life isn't about finding yourself. Life is about creating yourself.

— George Bernard Shaw

First, they ignore you. Then they ridicule you. And then they attack you and want to burn you. And then they build monuments to you.

— Nicholas Klein

The higher we soar the smaller we appear to those who cannot fly.

— Friedrich Nietzsche

Do what you can, with what you have, where you are.

— Theodore Roosevelt

To be yourself in a world that is constantly trying to make you something else is the greatest accomplishment.

— Ralph Waldo Emerson

This above all; to thine own self be true.

— William Shakespeare

Keep away from people who try to belittle your ambitions. Small people always do that, but the really great make you feel that you, too, can become great.

— Mark Twain

We know what we are, but know not what we may be.

— William Shakespeare

It's no use going back to yesterday, because I was a different person then.

— Lewis Carroll

If you think you are too small to make a difference, try sleeping with a mosquito.

— Dalai Lama

Trust yourself. Create the kind of self that you will be happy to live with all your life.

— Golda Meir

We are what we repeatedly do. Excellence, then, is not an act, but a habit.

— Will Durant

MOTIVATION AND INSPIRATION

Motivation is when your dreams put on work clothes

— Benjamin Franklin

· • — — · ✣ · — — • ·

Nothing can stop the man with the right mental attitude from achieving his goal; nothing on earth can help the man with the wrong mental attitude.

— Thomas Jefferson

· • — — · ✣ · — — • ·

Never stop dreaming, never stop believing, never give up, never stop trying, and never stop learning.

— Roy T. Bennett

· • — — · ✣ · — — • ·

If your actions inspire others to dream more, learn more, do more and become more, you are a leader.

— John Quincy Adams

Start each day with a positive thought and a grateful heart.

— Roy T. Bennett

Never lose hope. Storms make people stronger and never last forever.

— Roy T. Bennett

He had made himself believe that he was going to get well, which was really more than half the battle.

— Frances Hodgson Burnett

A professional is one who does his best work when he feels the least like working.

— Frank Lloyd Wright

Nothing comes from doing nothing.

— William Shakespeare

The best is yet to come.

— William Shakespeare

The best things in life make you sweaty.

— Edgar Allan Poe

We are all in the gutter, but some of us are looking at the stars.

— Oscar Wilde

The Will to Win

If you want a thing bad enough
To go out and fight for it,
Work day and night for it,
Give up your time and your peace
and your sleep for it

If only desire of it
Makes you quite mad enough
Never to tire of it,
Makes you hold all other things tawdry
and cheap for it

If life seems all empty and useless without it
And all that you scheme and you dream is about it,

If gladly you'll sweat for it,
Fret for it, Plan for it,
Lose all your terror of God or man for it,

If you'll simply go after that thing that you want.
With all your capacity,
Strength and sagacity,
Faith, hope and confidence, stern pertinacity,

If neither cold poverty, famished and gaunt,

93

Nor sickness nor pain
Of body or brain
Can turn you away from the thing that you want,
If dogged and grim you besiege and beset it,
You'll get it!

by Berton Braley

The best way to enjoy your job is to imagine yourself without one.

— Oscar Wilde

Do Something Now. If not you, who? If not here, where? If not now, when?

— Theodore Roosevelt

Opportunity is missed by most people because it is dressed in overalls and looks like work.

— Thomas A. Edison

· • — — · ✤ · — — • ·

Live it Down

Has your heart a bitter sorrow?
Live it down.

Think about a glad tomorrow
And live it down.

You will find it never pays,
Just to sit, wet—eyed, and gaze
On the grave of vanished days —
Live it down.

Have you made some awful error?
Live it down.

Do not hide your face in terror,
But live it down.

Look the world square in the eyes;
Go ahead as one who tries
To be honored ere he dies.
Live it down.

by Anonymous

· • — — · ✤ · — — • ·

If you're going through hell, keep going.

— Winston Churchill

· • — — · ❖ · — — • ·

Act as if what you do makes a difference. It does.

— William James

· • — — · ❖ · — — • ·

Learn the rules like a pro, so you can break them like an artist.

— Pablo Picasso

· • — — · ❖ · — — • ·

Never stop dreaming,
never stop believing,
never give up,
never stop trying,
and never stop learning.

— Roy T. Bennett

· • — — · ❖ · — — • ·

He Fails Not

He fails who climbs to power and place
Up the pathway of disgrace.
He fails not who makes truth his cause.
Nor bends to win the crowd's applause.

He fails not, he who stakes his all
Upon the right and dares to fall.
What though the living bless or blame.
For him the long success of fame!

by Richard Watson Gilder

You never fail until you stop trying.

— Albert Einstein

It is never too late to be what you might have been.

— George Eliot

Yesterday's home runs don't win today's games.

—Babe Ruth

· • — — · ♣ · — — • ·

Although the world is full of suffering, it is full
also of the overcoming of it.

— Helen Keller

· • — — · ♣ · — — • ·

But I know, somehow, that only when it is dark
enough can you see the stars.

— Martin Luther King, Jr.

· • — — · ♣ · — — • ·

You were born with wings, why prefer to crawl
through life?

— Rumi

· • — — · ♣ · — — • ·

Life is a shipwreck, but we must not forget to
sing in the lifeboats.

— Voltaire

· • — — · ♣ · — — • ·

98

A ship is safe in harbor, but that's not what ships are for.

— John A. Shedd

Even if you are on the right track, you'll get run over if you just sit there.

— Will Rogers

Imagination is everything. It is the preview of life's coming attractions.

— Albert Einstein

We either make ourselves miserable, or we make ourselves strong. The amount of work is the same.

— Carlos Castaneda

If you want to be happy, be.

— Tolstoy

· • — — · ♣ · — — • ·

When you arise in the morning think of what a privilege it is to be alive, to think, to enjoy, to love.

— Marcus Aurelius

· • — — · ♣ · — — • ·

You'll never find a rainbow if you're looking down

— Charlie Chaplin

· • — — · ♣ · — — • ·

Excellence is never an accident. It is always the result of high intention, sincere effort, and intelligent execution; it represents the wise choice of many alternatives — choice, not chance, determines your destiny.

— Aristotle

· • — · ♣ · — • ·

Wishing

Do you wish the world were better?
Let me tell you what to do.
Set a watch upon your actions,
Keep them always straight and true.
Rid your mind of selfish motives,
Let your thoughts be clean and high.
You can make a little Eden
Of the sphere you occupy.

Do you wish the world were wiser?
Well, suppose you make a start,
By accumulating wisdom
In the scrapbook of your heart;
Do not waste one page on folly;
Live to learn, and learn to live.
If you want to give men knowledge
You must get it, ere you give.

Do you wish the world were happy?
Then remember day by day
Just to scatter seeds of kindness
As you pass along the way,
For the pleasures of the many
May be ofttimes traced to one.
As the hand that plants an acorn
Shelters armies from the sun.

by Ella Wheeler Wilcox

Always dream and shoot higher than you know you can do. Do not bother just to be better than your contemporaries or predecessors. Try to be better than yourself.

— William Faulkner

Nothing great was ever achieved without enthusiasm.

— Ralph Waldo Emerson

Luck is what happens when preparation meets opportunity.

— Seneca

Our life is what our thoughts make it.

— Marcus Aurelius

For myself I am an optimist — it does not seem to be much use to be anything else.

— Winston S. Churchill

I never said it would be easy, I only said it would be worth it.

— Mae West

Shallow men believe in luck or in circumstance. Strong men believe in cause and effect.

— Ralph Waldo Emerson

Do not stop thinking of life as an adventure. You have no security unless you can live bravely, excitingly, imaginatively; unless you can choose a challenge instead of competence.

— Eleanor Roosevelt

Nothing is permanent in this wicked world, not even our troubles.

— Charlie Chaplin

· • — — · ♣ · — — • ·

No act of kindness, no matter how small, is ever wasted.

— Aesop

· • — — · ♣ · — — • ·

Attitude is a little thing that makes a big difference.

— Winston S. Churchill

· • — — · ♣ · — — • ·

The fishermen know that the sea is dangerous and the storm terrible, but they have never found these dangers sufficient reason for remaining ashore.

— Vincent Van Gogh

· • — — · ♣ · — — • ·

A hero is no braver than an ordinary man, but he is brave five minutes longer.

— Ralph Waldo Emerson

The most important decision you make is to be in a good mood.

— Voltaire

Difficulties strengthen the mind, as labor does the body.

— Lucius Annaeus Seneca

Keep your eyes on the stars, and your feet on the ground.

— Theodore Roosevelt

Instead of cursing the darkness, light a candle.
— Ben Franklin

When you arise in the morning, think of what a precious privilege it is to be alive — to breathe, to think, to enjoy, to love.

— Marcus Aurelius

· • — — · ✤ · — — • ·

If you enjoyed this book, I would be grateful for a review. These matter more than you might think.

• • • • • • • • • • •

If you would like to get in touch with me, please send an email to:

OldTownPublishing@Gmail.com

I'd love to hear from you.

INDEX

More books from
Old Town Publishing

Jonny Katz

*Now, That's Interesting: A Collection of
Fascinating Facts*

1,500 Weird, Wacky and Fascinating Facts

True Stories and Fascinating Facts: 1950s

True Stories and Fascinating Facts: 1960s

*Attention Curious Kids! Random and
Interesting Facts*

Miranda Powell

Word Jumbles: 100 Quotes by 20 Badass Women

The Office Crossword Puzzles

The Fabulous 1950s: Themed Crossword Puzzles

*The Unofficial Friends Word Search, Jumble, and
Trivia*

For Full List
Visit: https://OldTownPublishing.com

Made in the USA
Coppell, TX
29 December 2022

10021432R10069